M

Antony Rowland

M

Arc
PUBLICATIONS
2017

Published by Arc Publications
Nanholme Mill, Shaw Wood Road,
Todmorden OL14 6DA, UK
www.arcpublications.co.uk

978 1911469 16 2 (pbk)
978 1911469 17 9 (hbk)

Cover image:
'No 1 Spinningfields' © Colin Taylor
by kind permission of the artist

ACKNOWLEDGEMENTS
'The Siege of Minorca', 'Libya', 'The Natural History of Cock-
roaches' & 'Liberty Street' received the Manchester Poetry Prize
in 2012 and were featured on the competition site at http://www.
manchesterwritingcompetition.co.uk/Poetry-Prize.php.
The following poems have been published in journals and
magazines: 'Maria and Elizabeth Brontë', 'Verity's Tong', 'Heb-
den Bridge C.C., 1911' & 'MOSI' (*Stand*); 'The Knott Sluice' (*The
Wolf*); 'Rubber', 'Goitside' & 'Newark' (*English*); 'Prodromal' &
'Petty Cury' (*Poetry and Audience*),'The Jarls' (with the title 'Lin-
coln'), 'Brancaster', & 'St Jude' (*New Walk*); 'St George's Fields'
(*Shearsman Magazine*).
'The Knott Sluice', 'Tippler Weir', 'The School of Business' &
'Cheetham' featured alongside the artist Colin Taylor's work in
the exhibition catalogue for the *Cityscapes / Wordscapes* exhibi-
tion at Contemporary Six Gallery in Manchester in July 2015.

Editor for the UK and Ireland:
John Wedgwood Clarke

CONTENTS

M

THE SIEGE OF MINORCA

Europe ripples around this island
with Egyptian vultures, patient as the siege
of Fort Sant Felip, where I, John Murray –
our future as thin as Minorcan garrigue –
muster Lepanto and Xorigeur gin.
After Canavall and Canavant factions in Maó,
the road was paved with Kane's wine and seed
until the lynching of Admiral Byng
pour encourager les autres. Now the red globe
is a bleb on cannon exits to the sea
and our former deep water anchorage.

The stone curlew's reptilian eye catches
and holm oak, dwarf palm and carob
withhold their sap. My dream fevers
are of *sepia, fresas* and *gambas*
where anchovies torture the headland.
The bee-eater bubbles its pruuk
among barrack graves open from dawn 'til dusk.
The Tramuntana buffets with spicy wind
as clouds patch our mud. Nights draw meteorites.
Dim torches cast my death in momentary snow.

LIBYA

Economies brake on the crude prices,
the complicity of Libyan oil:
meet me at the reception of the water point,
the pump kid fuelled with Maserati dreams
where clouds form like afterthoughts above the logs,
coal and petroleum spirit. The office,
spick as a PIN, attends your balance and rewards.
Tubes anticipate the wireless pumps:
the nozzle pipe sucks air to a vacuum
before the clip click, fills with the corpses
of fossils compressed with mud and sun
then heated and cracked in refineries
to grades of kerosene and diesel pumped
for invisible trucks that fuel the night.

Jul 9th, 1755
Gleads kite the Saxon meers and marching hoopoes breed
but streams yield nothing but bull's head or miller's thumb;
the teams of ducks, widgeons, and multitudes of teal;
owls like dogs that hide what they cannot eat.
Three gross-beaks in my fields in the dead season,
shot with my dreams of swallows on the Isle of Wight
instead of cock snipes piping and humming to seed.
I have had yet no opportunity of procuring mice.

Aug 1st, 1759
I pass the trappers and thrusters with loaded corves:
I had rather look than go in pulpits. I write
rain, ecstatic as a solo. The hood-mould
shows water on the bulwark's central mullion
but the covert of eminence is truly beech,
most lovely of forest trees: glossy, pendulous,
beyond unmellow clay and crumbling black malm.
It seems the bees do not resent my large speaking trumpet.

Jul 14th, 1789
The Saxon's wolf-month: the floor sweats in wet weather
and when the lavants flood, corn will be expensive.
The blattae were almost subdued with fly-water,
surviving for weeks without heads. Tubbed and pickled
a fat porker, then culled some scummings for rushes.
Parties of ousels canton on the Sussex downs
and the goat-sucker or churn-owl jarrs on a bough
while the Bastille storms into history and Selbourne.

Macey's citified sprinklers cool models
working bikinis for your future jeans
while hawkers flog disaster off Broadway
with bites of images consuming the event
where the past is sky and prime estate:
these memorials' signature pools
are now clearly visible but do
not bring soil, cell cultures or snails
into Liberty Street. KERB YOUR DOG.
Hardhats snapple in annuated footprints.

No bushel experience here: the Staten lights
recede the ferry with its wake gulls past
Kioshk, Pagganck and Little Oyster
to an Island scrap-yard where the towers end
in a transferred zero of melted steel
and workers' tears. The bridge cinches the Heights.
In Bodies, full-on organs are preserved
in disturbing Chinese polymer-nerves.
Corporate headquarters shadow walkers
and Wall Street stiffens its Buttonwood lip.

Libeskind's wedge of light may yet not flood
pieces of high-heel shoes, a pair of metal,
as clear as the night is long. Span
the cables that spider the lattice to Ambrose
and Peking piers, the handshake
of Brooklyn. WE KNOW IT'S CALLED RUSH HOUR
but it is unlawful to cross the solid line
into understanding under NO STANDING.
Uptown, a trio of bald blue clowns
stretches the limits of performance art.

M

i.m. Kieran Crump-Raiswell, 1994-2013

I. PRODROMAL

Interpolate disinfectant:
the court pins families with light
and the defence barrister cuts
butter words: the defendant's face
is easy as a salesman,
suited and folded to pleas.
All stand for the nudge: jurors hawk
the statement change, his tongue wasting
into memory blank, banking
on the suit of psychiatry.
The brain floods with chemicals:
secrete the knife after the aorta;
upset your mouth. Welcome
to the Oast House: the jury's out
as thunder rounds its cloud
and the wake jars sound as a verdict.

ii. The Knott Sluice

Winter's spinning ice-markets trace
wonder beaches, *Furdustrandir*,
peeling from the lost river Dene
and Hanging Ditch, Irk to Irwell,
where the Hilton pummels a mansion
and water slops consumer dark.
Your label unease freezes,
cutting a tash down to the locks
with youth, with all your left to give
among arches, arcade bibbers,
varðlokkur chants in Piccadilly
under adverts' encomia,
ward enticers to the Etihad
past seborrhoeic road-dumps
and seasons without leaves:
sky blues dawn against Trafford reds.

III. TIPPLER WEIR

Trenches: your hold on these canals
where fry in dock wriggle to sump
far from the Rochdale *skraelingjar,*
the blush of Collyhurst sandstone.
A heron cramps. The pavements rink
in this *vicus*: a smithing hearth;
a poetry kiln. Metalwork
where horses tire the grassland.
A jackdaw crabs the guttering
where water thins the leaves down to
skin pits of dead walk *höfðingjar.*
You skirtled round the defenders
and planted it in the box. A tug
aspergillum sprinkles water.
Mills crunch Roman remains with clues
of cohort, word square, Mithras, culvert.

IV. THE NORTHERN QUARTER, ACUSHLA

Off traffic lights cluster their licorice
and a digger shackles its mesh
as the night tiles to your first pint
where scutchers honed cotton fibre
and a graduate plods a slab
torn as his suede. This since photo
has been bulldozed over nights:
The New Cross Labour Club, Ancoats.
Blinds hide the tired light that dusts
VOTE LATHAM: these pensioners doze
in best under the pole, proud
as flats that tower the canvas.
Now Homebase turns debates to scroll,
stamps flint glass, moss litter and
their politics hot as blossom.
May they have polled. May they piece rest.

v. The School of Business

Roofs soil with rain. Aerials
angle for spring, front after front,
as the window washes its evening
with percolating drops. Viruses
dry and prompt. Grim poetry,
not couth, you say – well then, live here
for twenty. Bounty in tyres
abandoned in an abandoned
garage. That hell dog yet again:
condition of sacks and meat slab.
Uni: BUSINESS AS USUAL,
though you made it your business to sack.
Sick of two cities after Kieran,
I packed away the recycling plant
and ignored the warning on my door:
THIS SPACE HAS BEEN RECONDITIONED.

vi. Sloid

Gloss the flood of eight foot six
in 1862, the Irwell
losing its banks: waves plunder
the birds' sloid and tin-opened graves.
Bones leak into future allotments
as young coves spread with the gardens
and the viaducts pike Gothic
for a spell. Swell the times
to last year's cross-field cross
for you. Defenders seep. Sodden,
the magpies still hop the showers
as the steps drain themselves of grit
and the invisible goalposts
tilt into hoodies. Memory
on an open snib: the trees
parade and open their ghosts.

VII. SMEATON

Scamper down Pegasus Walk:
laughing cars surf the puddle kerbs
and a burnt convertible rusts
the old horse track. Footpaths
converge the campus and Smeaton:
smitten with analogue static,
we inserted diurnal videos.
The bridge is an inverted smile.
Former gauntlet roads pitch silence;
egg boxes pittering in hedges;
doodads; the sheen of wrapper plants.
Nagging at box-lit memories,
we can only screen you frozen,
glued to a blue shirt before games
lodged on the slate, smiling
at legends we can only trace.

VIII. CHEETHAM

for Colin Taylor

A palette knife inscribes skyline:
blue crams white stack. A mill hovers
sight-lines of building vertebrae:
diagonals sink the river
to Crumpsall, 'crooked piece' beside the Irk,
thegnage estate where Stephen Oake
– DC with a memorial
hated with a chisel and daub –
drips on the threshold, weighted
with the suspect he will stumble
under, the Underground ricin
and aborted Bourgas plot.
You cannot free the evening
as it paints its clouds with light
then settles into your frame:
there will be a kitchen knife.

ix. Blackley

Kveldulf among folly and pitch
in *blæcleah*, a dark clearing
where suits give way to needle-mulch,
stomachs high and implicated
in toffee apples, candy as resin,
youngsters fighting the ladders
for the skelter pits. Hens jounce pellets.
The zoo llama stink the rose walls
as you lose yourself in a pelt
by the pond scunge, breathy turf
under the trodden pines. This earth
might unearth collar-studs as secrets;
a hayfield wall or shieling.
Lost whistles crave an evening
of shape-shifters, troll, giants and scorn-pole.

x. ETIHAD

Bramble over the bank cones
where gardens sink with opal plum.
Ticket and pass over Autogas;
sycamores ripe with plastic fruit
that spread and park a Beeching curve,
chair dump, Ovoline lubricant
and Cosco chute as early void.
Corms split the Burnable Waste
and car art bumpers the natural,
dumfounded at the Possession Centre.
The Etihad spiders the East,
leaks into terrace prices
and seasoned tickets in this March
of pollen regeneration.
Pollarded trees spike the heat.
Late and gone, the nettle rails.

A postcode only to conjure
and yet can spell you to centre,
aggressive stroke on a nightmare pitch
where you nibble the break and lounge,
a smile as long as we were off.
Clued into the geometry of slip
and gully, your ball fizzes
to stump. Supple as lime-wood
you gangle your youth to track:
a turning break spins the console
of words. Brood instead
on the clouds glutted with snow.
We're out: outside the frozen house
flakes twist in the panes' air.
Cars leave husks in the drift,
and gable warmth blackens our slate.

XII. CLAYTON LUNG

Bexwic: fresh eyes for my back teeth
as rain nettles the town and webs
our clocks. You ease your quietness
into lung canals, the sky
heavy with overlap, Aytoun
as limestone that dazzles like flake
where chimneys hold. A lift palette
oranges the controlled sunset
and psilocybin in colour rise
in Opinshawe, an open wood
or coppice. Why is it
always the East? Exhaust the fumes
with your breath and then lock
onto grid buddleia as hope,
these poets of the ringway,
bushing over the violence.

XIII. Grindlow Marsh

The byways of weed and silence
where Tai Pan sums the graduands
in the footsteps of your paintings
without rain: the stroke of Beetham,
Jain temple and Church of Pokrov
with its promise of Pentecost.
A torched bin tars to can sculpture
and barbies sputter their chicken.
Your skies are brush in lead faces,
the rush in a people-less square
where a LET BY leans to empty Benson.
Kieran's knapsack ghosts the screen
as the car hovers its attack, caught
in this oil and acrylic,
industrial states of mind
and the linen of heat and smog.

XIV. XCALIBRE

Outdated dishes winkle flats
and the litter thickens. Some of
the greatest fighters were poets:
Egil, Gisli, Grettir, Viglund,
now Solvi Chopper in the turf wars
between Gooch and Cheetham, fatalities
in water butt and thermal skin.
A blackbird shadows its flight to
the sun pipes of infusion homes.
Chopper pits in the Nico Ditch,
leaving the rich's stickiness
on leaf and plate, for his honour
and obstinacy. Meanwhile
garden into an apple orchard
where ox-eye daisies push their beds
and insulation regenerates.

XV. None need stay unless they wish

Graves bed the Mancunian Way:
Evensong will be said, NOT sung
where students hip prospectus grass.
Absent: the fundamental beard
of All Saints Church, topped in the Blitz
with its prayer books licking the flame
while the chancel coughs with smut
and the nave levels soot confetti
on the choked weddings. Pews hinge,
hoard boards pillaged hard by
UMAMI, bespoke octopus,
sliced to board the sushi rice
for what we are about, wasabi.
Waiters attend to table ends
rigid as your budding plum
that rigs the churchyard as you.

XVI. THE LAST PYLON

Our winter's redwings choke
the hawthorns, nesting
with cellophane clear as memory
as we nestle our flowers
to spot: cards shrink to pistils;
take weight at the second
funeral. Opposite, a bus stop
still boards the congregated pain
with a topography of gum
that snows the whole bay. Stemmed
with grief, the bunches are wiped
after an indecent interval,
berried to serenade Whalley Range
with chrysanthemums of the dead
by revellers, heading lovers
off at the Bass with pelted lilies.

XVII. DUMPLINGTON

Industrial Cerberus:
an anchor hooks the sky, borders
Wharf End and a culled history
of deer, lagoon and peat
where swings pool over the grebes.
Pulled after a price buck, a doe
tended the Tenax circle. Cancel
these palimpsests, or think on
the lost entrance at Throstle's Nest
and an ornamental lake boating
with our waste. Escalators
are treading the heath as war oil
expresses the lamps in Dumplington:
spot the eider in roundabouts.
Showers are rumours in footfalls
of the Centre's rococo and late baroque.

XVIII. Lensome's Island

Dead lavender blackens its patch
on Leofwine's holm, Viking island,
where plastic crusts the thistle stops
and a storm plays to a bow hum,
ricochets legato rain, bandwidth
after bandwidth. The irises
of Peter Lorre bulb the killer's *Schmerz*
compared to your light eyes,
a phone surface cool as your need,
your mute appeal to the gallery.
Your thoughts glue like cello strokes
as your sentence lengthens to shadow
and you pray for the chaplain.
Ash to orange and surgery:
late in Alexandra Park
the lake slides its mandarins.

XIX. THE PLUMAGE LEAGUE

Yukka tips speak of hotter palms:
you cannot prune with abandon
in Didsbury; litter expands
in rings of cup and take. Cars
point away: January
struggles into height where panels
suck for clean heat, renewable *amor*
as the bus stalls and jams language
at the stop where your ear strings
were unravelling the pavement.
Smeared with appetite,
the evening scarps your former bar:
our pints subdue the annual
like Hogni and his vats of ale,
and I can only slow the trees
as the gardens skew with rain.

xx. Coelfrith's Farm

Pedal liners strap the branches
and jalopies stack the yard
where snowdrops blanch the winter bark
and the ice-lake crepitates. No portents
in the footage, your white strings still
ghosting the black; and yet you want to touch
without touching for a hairline chat
as the dawn spills the allotments
where Martledge diggers dug marl and turf.
Your headphones took some moments.
Mourning is like getting a train
to the same station: LOOK BOTH WAYS
at macular degeneration.
The moon burrows through cloud. Birds
circle new elements as frost
leavens the pane with trilobites.

XXI. THE WITHY TREE

Snug as a winter ptarmigan,
Egil digests the *sceaga*:
rat-runs cut the terraces
like Icelandic sounds; Offerton sand
humps a drive where narcissi
break the freeze. Crocuses
fleck the park as these March clouds
spring their winter on pulling dogs.
Is this poetry as emolument,
my own Balke as Manchester,
the elegy as jalousie,
panhandling family grief?
Sleet drags its queue and fishmongers
are iced with scrod. Wythenshawe:
the paint fakes your memory
as the ides burn your Tudor stack.

XXII. BAGULEY

Bagca, badger, *Leah,* wood:
where they slap you into Christmas veins,
the gardens soak their marrows, and
beef chines and fritters glue their plates.
Outside the hall, they tend the plums
of Wheeler's Russet and Oullins Gage
while the master tilts in the tiltyard:
his muscles range as hammer-beams.
Martins announce their nests; keepers
prepare a wet larder for carp,
goose and beaver. The roses are cured.
The hammer-beam webs. You arrive
after weeks of the pox and blight
behind a scream and pinafores:
your dad leans like a whistler,
now umpire at your breathless head.

XXIII. Tonge Hall

Paintings   emblazon   fulfilment
     as evasion   dead   as the tarp
of *Mon Droit.*   You surround   our lord:
     treaties   sweetmeats   Flodden archers
the turns   and sleights   of prelatry;
     supplication.   You hang   your words
and pray   for settlement   as deer
     roam   for their arrows.   Imps
hang   the courtyards   and gloze
     like bench-whistlers   well-heeled
in insignificance.   I
handle the pike   and ponds   that Henry troughs
     for England.   Clouds plume   their red
under   the supplication   of
the terrace   the privy chambers
of our commerce   and grief.

35

XXIV. SIMISTER

The dew uploads redcurrant, but
we open the window louder
as a Semtex axle rises
to a roof. I cannot find a stop;
a postbox reddens and holds
the blast mailed to the centre
circling a memorial plaque
while a letter melts to silence.
At that moment you were a round.
Now litter the crush dummies
and freshen the air cuttings: these pubs
will move their stilts; these yards
like 80s brac and fruit arcades
will disappear as flats.
The walls jigsaw graffiti patch
as mist clings to a kraal of tape.

XXV. STONECLOUGH

Mesolithic activity
in *read clif*: from an axe-hammer
to whitsters and bleachers, a goit
powering the throstle-spin. Coal
reveals a breach at Ladyshore,
the exposed seam a revenant
to the hush shops of cock and bait.
Regret losing you for two
and why are we in Gainsborough
or in a Gainsborough, the stack
rumping over the coves and carts?
Spike, stump and memory pegged
to our futures: the foxgloves mourn
Hapag-Lloyd as outsize bricks
as the stop-loop weeds in Trafford Bar
and swifts depress their July Brexit.

XXVI. GORTON

We meet the thread of January:
the pavement iced to your fall,
a catkin in your face window
as the bus inflates. Switch your account
to laburnums, lichen and husk
on shelter trays of JC Decaux.
You know the fall of her style
the way that Audi ruckles its damage
where Salford gangs scuttled in peat
and the dirty Gore discoloured brooks
by the iron monastery.
Then *éla með meitli,*
a chisel of sudden hail
where he drove, slipped and feinted,
where you tore your earphones
to this arrow pinned on our map.

KIVERTON

i. The Jarls

A cathedral inks the distance
and the pavements tessellate and boil
their hypocausts, where a milestone
now commas a pipe. At Cardyke
the road buries feet under road and sinks
relics in the cellars at Clasketgate.
Thegns and jarls crowd their fires,
and wipe old soldiers like Celts.

Clouds paste the café ceiling:
a man satisfies his beer, then necks
a fifty at the toll booth
after the *duritia* of a Roman way,
a ruler between centurians' pain.
Knotweed flowers cellophane.
A bee wipes its images
where birches stream the Langsett gullies.

ii. Brancaster

Samphire needles the whelk track:
a wind break pulls its stones, and yurts
glamp the campsite with eco pods.
Crabs pincer the shallows as
a current rips the Holkham bar.

Partridges fritter the cured lawns:
we are a brace of peasants here
in Sandringham, where game heads spite
the queue through guns of state. We trounce
a sprinkler like a skipping rope.

A cove runs into secret reeds:
the baffle walls and a spinney
plug the pits that swell victims,
the smugglers of Geneva tea
who haunt the marsh with contraband.

Lopped artichokes purple the wreck:
spoon a cockle tub while rain
chunnels the Brachiopods.
Admirals glue the lavender,
as the Nene bulges at Tydd Gott.

iii. St Jude

The sea pictures rage their TVs
as lorries plumb the roundabouts:
the upstairs of a bus is canned
and a teenager in a shiftless home
leaves a mattress hemmed with a roof,
innocent leaves pinioned in space
as beeches haul their gravel slabs
that drivers nudge and peel around.
I wake, lungs raw, and check the crack:
the car is only dashed with rain,
the edge of Jude now chunnelling,
tearing the stickle-brick fens,
turning a blind tithe to
the burnt stubble of Lincolnshire.

IV. POOLE'S CAVERN

Buxton, 1454

Stalagmites poach with Grinlow lime:
I squint the rainbow candlelight
as limestone drops a platelet wall
with galena and fluorspar veins.
Rain erosion moulds sandstone caps
as the Law sniffs about the Peak:
guilt like a rimstone pool or gour
recalls my flashing, the grinding
of silver flakes to reform coins.
Among my amphorae fragments,
frogs pulse into hibernation;
moths cocoon over calcite winters.
I cheek the curtain rock and watch
gritstone edges erode my passage
and water twist through swallet caves
past scratched tourists named with a W
to ward spirits from the infant Wye.
My nest petrifies: minutes drip
to a gibbet or boulder choke.

v. We are sorry to announce

Up Steep   unleavened cathedral   under bare aisle
platform to hold   the sun   slicking the diesel   buffer squeal
buffering   the afternoon derailed   by goods   the points
Gainsborough   – sky, bench and stasis meet –   between call and cleat
a train multiplies   between counties.

Waiting moon passenger   minutes' thrift   tome weight
tanned October   Indian compensation   looped hills
into the plunge   of slope and city   the envelope scars.

Hut halt   weed lines   truck-palms flatten   to a bumper magnet
cob buzzards   increase to vanish   ash fluctuation   popped
allotments   bovine sit-in   oaks haunt   the pedalos
sheep biscuit   pelts a drowned barge   under-scraped tail kites
flash tractors attend   mags pile   magpie luck   dogslip
to Homebone   nettle containers   concentrate the grebes   Wem
support the lawn blowers   sun-strop   sprinkler plains   light peels
to chin   if these fields could break   livestock parking
ticket tool   the Maltings clamps   its grain   Morris clock
lubricants y Trallwag   cud bunch   soaks the night.

43

vi. Rubber

The Northern Rubber Factory, Retford,
where polymers of isopreme, the glands
and nubs of caoutchouc are pulped to bilge,
sticky as the taps from the Pará tree,
and its galvanised spouts knocked into bark.
Pustules are blobbing on the mashing slabs
as efficient bulbuls pump the churns
that run into Thrumpton Lane, cooling
erasers for future maths. Proteins
sequester at the surface particle,
sensitive to ozone-cracking equations,
the ribbed perfection of an orgasm
that never was, feathery as granite.
Light monsters stretch to the kids' cartoon
with bending ratio and kinky resistance.
Wrinkled conformations furrow Drayton
where this latex costume is confused
with the elastica of sex in Saxilby:
rubber as simultaneous turn-on and cough,
as outrageous as a super-hero
flashed in a diner selfie. Coconuts
are in abundance in Kerala now
after a hard day's rubber yakka:
cut lumps foam Kiverton until its bridge.
Crack cack-handed and it's bolted, this glue
tortured by children's arms, this pervert
of Westminster culls, this lettuce of spurge.

VII. Newark

Chillax patsy with your fib pasty,
you try to buy kudos from a mind stall,
class largesse with the Beast of Bradford
on Newark North Gate seeking a Cornish:
do you flaunt your flaky walls on a pendolino,
gristle mince between your incisive incisors
in an onion-soaked delight, gravy gunged
beyond gelatine in a comfortable sack,
laugh at the possibility of stilton,
admire the chock of corner potato,
swerve a burn nibble devoid of filling,
pastry like a kiss without the squeeze
of lava cheddar or liver spills; or admit
to an order years too late? You are caught
in the floodlights of a forecourt, after
the pumps are hooked, plying a Ginster,
the flab of cellophane and its meat sludge.

Gorge instead on custards dipped in vanilla,
entreat your cousin Otter to express venison – which is,
    true to form, palpable beef
(not handsome, says Pepys) –
or binge on in-it-together jumbo sausage.
Learn from the Pasty Fest in Calumet,
Mexican paste in the state of Hidalgo,
Jamaican patties that shell the turnover,
Spanish empanadas quenched with fruit
and briks, pelmeni, ubiquitous samosas.
Or let there be, simply, some dainty Pork-Pye.

Take your spigarnel of spayne and break it
in a pot of good ale, where Eric his aching girth
would span/ And roar above his pasty pan.

Pudding Lane is burning down burning down burning down
The fleis und fisse pasty was refined in its fission
Quando fiam uti the cram of turnip? O swallow swallow
I sold my comforter to Billy Blake for a wortleberry pasty
These pasties I have shored against my ruins
Why then I'll brown you and your suet.
Flagons of hock and delicate ionckettes.

      Pasty   pasty   pasty

VIII. I CHANGED IN SHEFFIELD

I changed in Sheffield and ate an awful pie
I changed in Sheffield and ate rain
I ate Sheffield and changed a pie
I changed at Sheffield and ate stationary
You are what you change at Sheffield
The state of Sheffield is an awful pie
Eat pies and change yourself into Sheffield
Peter Piper picked a peck of Sheffield pies, and died
Sheffield is changing into an awesome size
Size 14s shouldn't change at Sheffield
I charged at Sheffield with only a pie
I entered Costa Coffee with the sole intention of choosing a
    pie, but was trickled the treats of blue muffins, muffins
    like flies' cemeteries, a cross between muffins and food,
    fair-trade chocolate and several varieties of maltesers,
    biscuits, biscotto, totty wafers and a large mug of jam,
    but nothing pie-like, no tart offering, tartin-gaping or
    even a flat torte, so I left.
I changed at Sheffield and Norwich opened up to me in
    this can of oozing passengers, too sad to be late
Change 'I' into Sheffield to underline personal tragedy
I changed in Sheffield when the south turned to mizzle
I changed Sheffield into a metaphor due to electrical work
I turned Doncaster into Tenerife, but only on Sundays
Beware the sliding platforms of your wet creams
Due to the jet conditions, please trail the vapour of your
    neighbour's cigarette
Due to the net timing of your journeys, please despair
    under this arrow
Change platforms to miss connections at will
Only connect your legs to the bridge during maintenance
The sky caved in when I boarded a diesel unit

47

Change to the slow train of Hope Valley, where Kinder
  Scout sucks cloud and New Mills trains the precipice
Slow the axles to flood the moor, the tractors down with
  unfathomable sheep, spilled onto cabbages
Or just stay in Sheffield forever
Marry a platform and eat a midnight track
I changed in Sheffield and ate an awful pie

THE ROAD OF AMERCIAMENT

1. GOITSIDE

What is the source of Allerton beck, or
the ash barrows on Rombalds Moor? Home
in a sootless bowl: a valley ruttles the chest
of Mudpuppy town where we, goats dressed as mutton,
hit the gown. Rain pips the new clearing
in Jacobs Well. Moss clogs at Thistletake
for which payment, all rearing swine
shall feed the wood of the Lord in the time of Pannage
when swine gorge on acorns and wild fruit.
De-vine to depot entry: trams hum
and ballet cranes spindle the car pyre.
Gas binds in Mills Hill Malta factory
weaving to high-visibility locks,
turbine Pennines loco, and the Rochdale clock
locked at one, the time of unscrupulous men
whose sordid exactions provoked discontent
like crows' nests, crows *ober* the hills' pillion,
common pastures for the common. Have you
ever clocked in? Click a parkin pig
on the road of amerciament, the goit
of Lord Clifford, copped in an empty neck
with a headless arrow one moon before Towton:
the boucher of Wakefield, barbarian dispatch
killed by a bush. Don't mess with a Halifax thaw
when the banks slow with ice and mattress,
the cuttings husked with industrial stone
and OINTMENT, karlhaxes and pikestaves
daily arrayed in wyrehatt doublets
in this place so very full and populous,
this place so very factious and seditious.

II. Maria and Elizabeth Brontë

Pinchbeck fields close the back door:
Patrick moves through Flappit Springs,
lurches over the Worth and turnpike
to their last home, a peat room
among streams that break the valleys,
feeding their minds with hot bricks
where air exposes graves and sewage.

Educated in the foreign matter
of a stew, Maria and Elizabeth
are cooped, sewing the hours,
brewing consumption to an end
on the bend of the Leck and frost
in Cowan Bridge, where 'bingy' milk
dirties the pans in stair-rod rain.

Smell changes the rooms:
from burning to kin, the torture
of chilblains in Tunstall Church,
cold tongue to feed teeth chattering
the service with a Nankeen Spencer
and matching tippets, bonnets rimmed
to calico sermons and window sleet.

III. St George's Fields

Two of the author's relatives are buried on Leeds University campus. Leeds General Cemetery, which had become overgrown, was taken over by the university. Most of the gravestones were demolished to make way for a park in 1968.

In the soaked towns where the Pennines hunch,
terraces cling to absent glaciers:
Wellington's memorial pokes the thaw
but not forgetfulness, as a snow-line

packs against Slaithwaite and a dry-stone wall.
Mill ponds poach foam and defreeze in Batley
before the pull to the family bones
by the bleached library that stakes the hill.

WILLIAM ROWLAND peered over the soot
and gloom of Georgian stone, now enclosed
by Geography and its erasures,
my umbrella that spiders in the gale.

SAMUEL ROWLAND is flat round the chapel
like an afterthought: lucky at least
to ward even a daubed plot in Holbeck.
The gravestones pull away from the nave,

as my trainers smudge mud from windscreen names
after name. I pocket embarrassment
by a lodge and astronomical digs;
picture crushed stones returned to their quarry.

These gravestones were desecrated like teeth
extracted from the skulls below, quiet
as this rook that stands in for sorrow,
pitched in the crumble of marble saints.

Did diggers cut the cut names back to sand
and university hands tame bunches,
then rubbish the pin-cushion flower pots?
Only an advert in *The Yorkshire Post*

saved others. Even with a brother
in nearby Ganton Mount and a poet
burrowing Mercia and the blue wounds,
you were surplus, and required space.

The university is aggressive,
acquires majority shares and holds
stones at tibia length for contractors,
then designates the field's chapel as

special, of historical interest, more
architectural than working-class bones.
After, Somerset House loses the tombs,
and fire ticks the Bursar's photographs.

The remaining graves cluster the alders.
Visitors now pay homage to a sod:
death chunked the university's *Raum*
so it bulldozed the shade and lingerers.

The rich are stubborn in their sunken tombs:
GEORGE NUSSEY, late dyer of Bishopgate,
departed this life but not his text;
a circular angel whipped to a ghost.

Please Respect the Act of Parliament
for Quiet enjoyment and rest. Games
cannot be Permitted. Dogs must be lead
in the interest of Public Health and grass.

Cooperation of the dead would be
appreciated. Last year's leaves
log the spot, empty as their branch;
its path leads only to a public bin,

neoclassical grave turrets, twisted
and locked in an ever-expanding beech.
The sun is coined in fibula trees;
shines on petting, heavy with a lunchbox.

Soon hail pelts my sagging plastic and drips
as I crab past the haphazard years
of names: Washington followed by the thrush.
The weather of austerity: bitter

as the hand that takes and promises
we're all in it together; together
as this beneficent angel propped
on a bought grave saved from the yellow maw.

Mauve tops birth my wide occupation,
clamming mud from yet another year,
years before education could be bought
for a small mortgage, or a song for the rich.

A riveting Rowland line bucked by print
until the threat of the triple-dip;
the purge of Cameron's curtain scroungers;
the wealth of dagger cuts and generous tax;

the rupture of class and Daniel Jones
astounded at the Bullingdon Club.
We now know our place as William did,
a dream cobbler among the plough and bear

who couldn't even nail death with a stone,
who attended siling winters on roofs
of Leeds Grammar School, excused for nights
alone with the constellations of night

so long that his fingers, spidery hand,
froze into a clutch for his indentures.
Then, among the border creep, AM ROWLAND,
wiped into hiding through years of sedge.

WILLIAM ROWLAND rescued from slate
and desecration on yearly name-stones.
Somehow, among the hate, hangs Osborne's smile.
Competition is good: sell the dead

for bucks, our star-crazy cobbler, quick
as lime before the Leeds outcries, sullen
as ethics. Appreciate capital
and the approaching stripes that yell, BANKER!

The borrowed light in the carriage hides mist,
and the sun still gashes Warth mill and tow path.
The navvy walls cut and hang Marsden,
and birches draw silver from Polish sap.

We will shortly be arriving at deeds.
Dewsbury roofs float triangles; odd
horses dredge humps and black fields of lake.
Batley silage pits work their churn and fume.

iv. MOSI

Horse gins walk the coal tubs
in a Wakefield pit, until
water turns the Breastshot cogs.
    piston beams
    crank and flywheel
Manchester Galloways fire the world.

Steam fuels potato peelers,
chip fryers, drives mixers
and dough in bakeries.
    flannelette sheets
    ballwheel governors
chacking the pistons as the gas explodes.

The pressure of steam
jutters a bulb in these
displaced males in oil lotion.
    socking the valves
    driving the light
where my grandad bellows his hut in night.

Oil welds stopper clots,
splodges on can patina,
this nose of an anteater.
    treadle lathe
    drainage sough
nothing in the trap now but frozen blobs.

A spring pushes the air
as the decades pile in, scratched
to Hunslet with your stiff joints.
    moisture tester

click reel winder
all objects locked in their technology.

Memory swells kisses,
grain-tics lodged in the lubricate,
the chaff of a Wheaten tin.
        your pumice stone
        your stone bottle
the blotches like stories on your fine skin.

v. VERITY'S TONG

i.m. Hedley Verity, 1905-43

The gift of a barometer holds the toss
where Yorkshire means more than England
until the war. You harden arms
in the coal depot, your line a plumb bob,
happier on the flat than a sticky wicket
with red roses to be bowled
to Pudsey dentists. Last at Hove
where willow is leathered with talk
of Poland beyond the boundary of sea.

Cricketers' Owen, a week from leave,
weak from dysentery, stripping a Bren
with two right hands, consisting
of thumbs. Then the Catania guns, caught
plum in front of the Arno line:
gravestones range in flag patterns for
the score at Tong; your never-ending spell.

THE BARREL ORGANS OF ZEEDIJK

I. TAORMINA

i.m. Florence Trevelyan, 1852-1907

You turn the innocent ioponica
as English beaches shut like cliffs:
after bitter amaro you course
your garden of ashlar, recall
the pressed consort who kissed you
into stringcourses of volcanic stone,
the beautiful hole of Isola Bella
and this balustrade cutting outcrops
with your outrage; Balmoral mores
that sink your banishment
to a park of carved *apiari,*
beehives as cabins with closed birds.
Powerful diminishments:
tanked under the chamaerops,
your future Sicilian husband
crams at Padua, far from the pinea
where you pine for your fading son.
After, you are *'a 'ngrisa',*
the Englishwoman, adored
for your charity, walking with slippers
until you find your shoes. Aucuba Edward
shuffles into thoughts, a crown
and shucks your nights. *Vino
alla mandorla* presses your heart
as your view tightens the sand.

II. THE BARREL ORGANS OF ZEEDIJK

Grummets and rowlocks route the canal
into histories of packet and gable chain,
the pianos hoisted to drown
the sugar colonies and bloody lace.

Your dress clings to an open decade
as they kindle the sloping *boeken*
and tilt the houses to the Bechstein keys
of Kaisergracht. The sloe canal

pastes leaves as we waste Oktober bock
and crow our feet at Hagel Slag.
The best book since Shergar chooses
a needle passage smoked with grass

and copper like litter round cyclamen.
The drains feint at Westkerk: moving statues
ruin the cobbles as the train loses you
for chocolate and wasabi pastures,

ditches that stalk with egrets and polders
sunk like the teens in Arendsnest;
new refugees over costume pots.
Wind turbines stitch the ocean's thrill.

Opinions breakfast like standing water:
the reptiles of the mind ponder *Lebensraum*
then mulch the *Senf,* tossed with the health
of Gesundbrunnen schnapps and unfiltered beer.
The See complements the minutes. Now,
a metonymy of seats for absent goons,
forced lions and symmetry that hushes
the desk lamps and artificial rooms.

The *Schnauze* is suspicious of allee:
BMW tint blackens its driver.
Yachts stem and bell the wash: a crested grebe
suspends the algae. Cobbles anchor chestnuts
that swell the *Herbst,* and settle the needles.
Innocent tiles cling to the fudge
of plaster: blue windmills accord a shriek;
'schrecklich' repeats a man, who sees nothing.

Immaculate cubicles poise their flush;
kick steps wait in library aisles.
Take me to the neurosis of platforms
where mikes glued to the eve of conversations
dropped miles away in the strip. 'Protect
all Covert Objects' sold with Euro cakes.
The king's bridge opens the sky to view
MIELKE in red on the Wannsee front.

IV. ÜSKÜDER

for Omar Pamuk

The city owns our centre:
carp spotlights like ghosts
to Medusa stones, the stone tread
of snakes and underwater dreams,
cream boats shelled at night
for weddings. You move
among chipped frescoes,
Justinian domes floating space
where Mehmet swept the relics
to carve a marble ambo.

Bright Eastern fantasies
of Marmara ships holding
the blue and mood as
piped Imams rush
through thinning air,
sound kites of Sultanahmet,
afternoon prayers suspending
the Efes? Or *hüzün*:
imposition on the Mihrab
and apse for the sultan's loge?

Fish crystals wink
and narcotics poke the lira.
Water pipes clean your evening mind
but your memoirs are lies
you said, and East does not meet West
yet buckets and sinkers
still wet the heat. Bazaar:
paprika and saffron
tub for wallets with lokum dice
and the pressure of Üsküder tea.

'When Nammouche was not singing, he was torturing'
NICOLAS HENIN

The Hôtel de Ville mocks a cathedral,
funnels its light to the weather,
breaks into cirrus where archangels
still stay a dragon. Revellers smudge
the photograph of the Place Royale:
a flagged statue stones his infidels,
singing from the plinth of history,
his folds of hair like a croissant knot.
From Syria to the Manneken Pis
then Sablon and cobbles, spayed with bullets:
a door freezes for its re-enactment,
the burden of event and wound.
A nervous plaque heralds its bronze
as memory floods the Grote spur.

VI. CANAUXRAMA AND INDEPENDENCE

Les enfants hammer the sand,
pit their tempers across handles,
as wasps move the sandwiches,
and a fountain recycles the afternoon.
We puddle through our water, where
the padlocks block the *pont* L'Archeveche
with its clutter of bolted love.
The canal trip locks its natives
with the water gauntlet of Canauxrama,
from L'Arsenal to La Villette
where the gate opens like a nation
to the Bastille marooned in traffic
through the charity touts chugging
from bridge to heart, and the hands
of bitter Maredsous: the citron
is as tart as your *au revoir*.

VII. Bar Hotel

The suburbs once flowed for reorganisation
where the sidewalks are still existing,
creating time to time and a bright deck;
once or twice, without a whimper
just before it was incurred. No one
regrets this procedure: this bar hotel
is on the verge of swirl, confused –
because it fits so well with our district.
The toilet can only be converted
for the purpose of a seat belt
to make of an aircraft seat was wrested.
Only pleases one's packed tight, but
we are only one in there, you have
the feeling to be very promising:
the people are a lack of available space.
Everywhere, everyone chatters with anyone,
problems with neighbours, all ears and noses.
'Do you ever at the window?', so
a voice is often heard and will then
have done well. Any puffs where he sees fit.
The bar hotel has retained some anarchy:
consumption is okay, but not as a focal point
for punks. Go see the plurality of like-life
in the face. The pub is run by others:
pick up language in an evening.
In the small place they einheizen hard:
hot it is in the basement of the gorgeous
and the DJ looks unlike Hank Snow, soul-vinylene
to the panting beats quality for cooking. Dance
should be absolute where respectable people are gathered:
the charm of secrets have some point there.
No concept: then Quentin Tarantino may be observed

here soon canoodling – and not in the established
local channel. May be anger is one or the other,
the next day on foul-smelling hair: direct your steps!

VIII. Dance Economic Kaffee Burger

In the basement there was a bakery,
until the ban on dancing in the early forties
was geschwoft in coffee houses, and of course,
again, as they spat in his hands. Later,
the upper floor was empty, used by the Stasi
as an observation post for the log haul hub.

In the seventies, the burger trendy bar,
which did not mean whatsoever 'scene'
was staying, but the master and walk-in customers
with more or less infamous creators permeated was.
In 1979 a large number of competent authorities
strongly advised to thoroughly, and thus in GDR
conditions lengthy renovation
to drain the cesspool of contention.
The 'scene' attracted to other angle bars –
what remained were the velvet wallpaper,
the sheet Muschebubu-light installation.
In the eighties, the burger was as full as troublemakers
even without any other DDR pub. In the nineties,
Mrs. Burger has held the position and prevented
from being Casinos, fine restaurants, hairdressers,
pharmacies and similar nest irrelevant.

In 1999, Karl-Heinz Heymann, landlord
of the premises for difficult cases
with the unusual name 'Winsenz' putzigerweise
brought the culinary under two operators,
the ex-UPS Field Marshal Uwe Schilling
and sealing the leather jacket Bert Papenfuss,
suffer long should. Papenfuss, in his spare time
writing meaningless founders, and shilling's old 'Slave Market'

were veterans looking for a new home for their lubricate
literary and small musical ambitions. They thought,
in a newly established shop would do everything better:
it was then, too, only worse.

After recently rebuilding the dance bar industry
Kaffee Burger opened the cultural program
was the stupid name 'Salon bridge head'
which was intended as a response to the salon
just rampant glut, served its purpose and fell oblivion.
Shortly afterwards, the former was Mrs Rest room
to the beer opened to the public. Since then, the quilted bear.
The rest is history, manners – which stretches.

THE END

Psephologists poll our defeat,
so hoard your vascular soil
as we abandon earth for burrow,
the ecosystem of a mole
in the mulch ball of a starship
where fish unbubble water tanks.
Sage circuits glitter like monitors
that tickle the plants as we fade.
Microbes laugh in your future place:
we starve on asteroids, space junk,
as oxygen falls with orgies
of roaches. We did not lack skills,
but synthetic dirt recycles our paste
as gravel pits level to age
and diamonds shape to our own end.

BERLINERMAUER

Panelled into oblivion in Metzer Eck, windowless pool subterfuge during my part in the Wall's downfall with breadcrumb-fired herring washed down with bortsch and Kelvin's chimpanzee: if the trams don't get you the bicycles will in frost sluice down the Berg to Kaffee Burger, flake painting replaced with flock wallpaper and unfiltered Bier after the bier of our evening. Drinks machines vend memory as we together it for Wedding, Bourne sirens

in Tacheles urine and 80s
squalls, ripped n' graffiti
old store doors impress us
not kiss-and-tell Polaroid
capital river now demoted
neoclassical hubris haunts
giddy youth leapfrogging
of Eisenmann, then losing
excitement among those
your *Currywurst* dreams
of an underground library
where the books ascended
a *pouvre* Libeskind then
hard by pork knuckle of
our *Kartoffeln* exploits
illuminates *Fernsehturm*
now. Tram tracks hitting
local cat-flap gravestones
hammered and chiselled

pop squat grunge tourist
bar grill idioculture more
than department store art
and yet another dam wall
to our corporate sledge by
pock-chipped Reichstag
to the undulating channels
each other in the loose
frost-crack patched stele
to sauce the source
lighting with absence
bluewards by the Oper
erects a culture palace
always the fried lardons
where the bruise sun
winters still scandalous
the night's Volkspark
flanking the mausoleum
among mourning Lindens

your eye-whites attract the room along with sensuous thumb jumper sleeves: order me about three unfiltered beers any day. Drunk loses the hang of bransticks, shares his sticky evening where tomorrow never flies because it is a capercaillie. Pen-air memorial portals for oral testimony against the morning flags, the time return from black stills, the regretted youth through the window, the hero who plans utopia, packs a fag packet, fingers Stalin and jumps

Bunkers: hill-top bastions now mazed in culture park innocence, the Karl-Marx-Allee-marked citizens on a wide utopia, no longer *Turm*-watched at Tränenpalast, the Palace of tears. Kreuzberg church sprouts a *boule* cupola to a foliage equal. Do we rush the Ampelmann, or just jay walk into terror? Sudstern didn't deign to *Dunkelbier*. I could have slapped the waiter's brain, but he made a good fist of our disappointment. But why all these

curtains after café doors
and *plaan* froth among
hemp markets for the 80s
of the Spree tributaries
the limestone Tempelhof
Speer art deco cloud
mothering of all airports
Dr Kendall's mathematics
clownish clown radio
take me to the *Halle* and
soon Libeskind shine
exiled in the Exile and
neoclassical shattering
confusion with forks
faces you shouldn't step
iron multitudes in voids
installation babble preen
totally discombobulated
just waiting my new *Turm*

step ladders to bar heaven
latte Euros, old West-hit
cold 'fuck you' altitude
new icons of Berlin kitsch
Halt shuddered in another
unexploded long quadrant
an equation held an airlift
this clown with one rather
juniper-rinsed *Sauerkraut*
survey the market plies
where no right angles
drunk with the degrees
again channels undulate
no windows to easytopia
Bobby stopped the clank
cling each other in the
lose the bunker concert
among the poppy strudel
in the old evening's 'yes'

cut down then the Potsdam *über*-European slack stop over the late frost Jannowitzbrücke, the taste of leaves, frozen air, the river thick with shadow, memory visits, your inner *Ossi*, welter of events held in the Pergamon oriels, museum columns in this jumble city, *Bitte ein Bit* of Bitberger bars, GDR *Ostalgie* speaks easy, into which I space this capercaillie, its display as wincing as my distressed denim and mid-life bicycle, its hen fluttered in embarrassment glue

Booked into conflict, Hotel Wartburg waited, brick by brick: its foundations collage into lego history; blocks point at the flowers' *décolletage*, towards the former bloc. This mortar is imperfectly preserved, its waiters lost in the shafts: Allied bombs carved below expressed paths of the *Flakturm*. Shafted with elevator absence now, it is elevated to grasshopper trees, bosky over the cool turns of the Autodrom, desire lines of old learners' erasures.

PLEASE DO NOT DIS
this artistic dereliction
until the rubble manicure
always piled upwards
kindling with the *Kind*
hosepipes could mean a
post as atom-holding
compressed as car sugar
lotions' rumbled theft
faring as gilded bath taps
of plaster, plastered nights
frozen into an ice-*Platz*
content with a rictus
officers tight in form
homing my pastry flight
sweating in the air-locks
walls capture their sound
o sweet *Honig* syrupy
peradventure corners
opposite trolly doilies
unwetted coffee pots
chiselled Stauffenberg
fired in Fromm squad
stripped to a statue
defying a plinth waste
pats on a reformed hand

the lacquered rocks
Trümmerfrauen warten
this Styrofoam beach-tip
ohne Zeichen, humane
firing, plying the valve
cleaning, *sauber* or fire
all those torched rallies
keys timed into scrap
shale-compacted affairs
sumped into crumb
glazed outside Europa
fingerlings to continents
polka officers, chap-stick
triangle udders of *Möjke*
the kludge of gelling
bricks singing the air
capitulation of breakfasts
Pfirsiche peppered *Bresse*
on Stauffenbergerstrasse
the old Benderblock
whetting the passers
defines the sticking place
Neupfadfinder scouts
unheeded trees, rain
naked in brain search
chained reliance

whereas his men have full pants and 'sawdust in their heads' as the plot is stricken. Sciamachy. As resistance falls, these *Köpfe* thicken to *Kerle*. Haeften, Quirmheim, Olbricht gather hastily in the armament pit; bequeath *Sippenhaft* as relatives quell towards Austria. Pictures of child strictures, pinafores of these stripped walls worried with glory. A sprint face hassles the *Damen*. A sandbox. Sand spit like a chalk shock on the western edge of Denmark.

A pornography of expectation only in *Tago Mago* as the can Astra files into Anne-Frank-Platz. A yellowhammer sings a headstone with bit bread and *keine Käse*, as horse flies count their welts. Hover-flies of pollen drift the sunshine soaked with grass, the mass graves bobbing with iPads. Augmentation across the pollenating weeds: a guard tower entangles your beard while the barracks cut wood words; the clouds with lost messages

a blur of roses, slopped
stumble testimony, photos
green highways of finch
the absence of a pit-doze
reserve nature on dog trot
lost in cold *Tropfen*
hocked on a soak plateau
the voice-app *dort drüben*
I feel only pockets
looming Lüneberg *Birken*
the danger to connect
weighing in dog ketchup
we might through people
refuse to juxtapose, tack
the typhus children,
sheets cannot frown the
motor still Richard
Dimbleby can we make
this live Anne Frank
Appelplatz, the Polish X

granite *Rühe* of stones
surface tablet *Düschen*
reveal little, a parkdam
such bulldozed realities
the lead to the goldfinches
the seeping *Nieselregen*
technology of the plotting
uninhabited excerpts each
you are birch-trapped
strops of memory, over
maybe thru *Senf* only
mumble sweet *Brödchen*
yet the obelisk politeness
you leave me a square
your eyes are separating
sound all installation gaps
tongue-stropped with hate
are we all failing to *sehen*
box installation gap-wires
krek-krek branches a kiss

The day's residue foments as I lose you in a paternoster shaft, a dream obscene in its lightness. Herb grass flosses over the tent camp, daisies among curated gaps. Play historical audio or haul in the thrushes, the hammers that range beyond GPS? Concrete: a clump trunk over a virtual tree and the *Schlüssel* point, the *Dampf* of a shower grove, the *Brod* that haunts the afternoons with a plastic edge, circling the perimeters. *Ja, gewiss*, but can I leave my bag?

Rust poles of Bernauerstrasse fish the sky: they could be the pre-*Wende* staves of the Wall but look too neat, if rightly hugging the line swerve to Nordbahnplatz and an overpriced bistro. Indie crowds blacken the past for the Flohmarkt on Mauerplatz and a *Glüwein* freeze after the end of daily life with dog runs and control strips, then commemorative landscape. The old East, crumbled to perfection, excavated for earthworks exhibitions of the

death strip coffee curtains	whisper among the lattes
cups before the brick café	Kohlhoff & Kohlhoff and
historic froth of guards	their tower rubble and all
entwines the recent doors	file up now the squirm
to survey the preserved	reconstructed archaeology
post guards plastered	with *echt* frost spiralling
onto the breathing flats	locked as memorials
we inserted eye slats	thereby the *Polizei*
could just peep past	domestic gatherings
kettles to stop the leap	spying maps and chains
suspending the cool fag	wire-jawed for camera
falling into capitalism	and its warm net but we
brush tarnished brass	the escape plaques
trodden and lonely	*Stolpersteine*, not brash
Hackescher Marckt	*Steine* deportation icons
stubbed with sole and butt	near the Ampelmann shop
Ostalgie can't airbrush	with pat Trabant kitsch
stray hatted Ampelmänner	walking into the red lights
of themselves who install	Alexanderplatz traffic

these slabs like a game memory, collected at the wrong angle by cemetery edge, dead slats engraving the gravitas of entrenched ideology, the building absurdity of moment jumping through back windows to the West, the human remainders of brick patch and forced evacuation, the inevitable holes of sewer mash, the subsequent police hunt sealed with a goose in Prater, *Schwarzbier* that buds my attention, this man, inside his car, who is washed

BIOGRAPHICAL NOTE

ANTONY ROWLAND's books include *The Land of Green Ginger* (Salt, 2008) – which was shortlisted for the Michael Murphy Award – and *I Am a Magenta Stick* (Salt, 2012). His poems have been anthologised in *Identity Parade: New British and Irish Poets* (Bloodaxe, 2010), and *New Poetries III* (Carcanet, 2003).

He received an Eric Gregory Award from the Society of Authors in 2000, and recorded for the national Poetry Archive in 2009, and the Lyrikline (Berlin) in 2014. He was awarded the Manchester Poetry Prize in 2012.

Antony has read in a variety of international settings, including Nijmegen (2015), New York (2011), Berlin (2009), Gdansk (2007) and Strasbourg (2002). The Dutch government elected him as a UK poetry 'ambassador' for 2016: his poetry was read on national television, and shown on screens at Schipol airport and Amsterdam Central Station.

http://www.poetryarchive.org/search/site/antony%20rowland

Titles in Arc Publications'
POETRY FROM THE UK / IRELAND include: